Use Your Haters As Escalators

Dr. FerRonnie Sampson

ACKNOWLEDGEMENTS

I am first thankful to GOD for allowing me this opportunity to share some of my life experiences with you, by way of writing this inspirational book. Without GOD, I am nothing. GOD is my true source for everything in life.

Secondly, I thank my mentor, pastor, and dad—Marion Sampson and my mom—Sylvia Sampson, who are such an inspiration to me. My parents are the main reason for my success. They taught me at an early age to always trust and keep GOD first and never give up on my dreams. I also thank my brother, Tyron, for the integral part he has played in my life.

More importantly, I am thankful for my most beautiful wife, Sharlene, who whole-heartedly supports me in all my endeavors. Sharlene is truly my best friend, a woman who encourages me and stands by my side every step of the way. I also thank my daughters for all their love and support.

In addition, I am grateful for the Breath of Life Faith Church family which is truly the greatest church in the world that has given me a platform to hone and develop my skills and has prepared me well to succeed in any career of my choice.

Finally, I thank all my Haters for motivating me to write this book! If it wasn't for your ridicule, insults, lies and disbelief, I would not have the courage to share my story.

In December 1997, I received my Bachelor of Science degree in Criminal Justice from the University of Maryland University College. In May 2001, I graduated from Bowie State University with an M.A. in Administrative Management and an M.B.A. in May 2004. In June 2007, I graduated from Taylor University (formerly "Fort Wayne Theological Seminary and Bible College") with a Doctor of Theology Degree.

My strong determination, persistence, and faith in GOD, have combined to fuel my desire to succeed in whatever task is before me. It is my prayer and belief that this book will be a blessing and encouragement to you and that you will, "Use Your Haters as Escalators."

SPECIAL THANKS

Special thanks to KDH, a dear friend, who chose not to be mentioned, but took the time out of his busy schedule to proofread my first inspirational book!

Special thanks to A"T"H, a close friend, who also chose not to be mentioned, but assisted me with formatting issues during the final book review!

APPRECIATION

I appreciate the phenomenal expertise of Andrew and Tiffani Gorbonos in creating the photo cover shots and assisting me with the wardrobe selections. For photography inquiries, please contact Andrew Gorbonos on the following website:

www.andrewgraydc.com

TABLE OF CONTENTS

Chapter 1

WHAT ARE HATERS?

Haters are simply people who (1) are jealous of you; (2) do not want to see you achieve any success; and (3) continue to discourage, distract, and do everything they can to keep you from reaching your goals and dreams. In other words, haters are born to keep you suppressed and make your life miserable. Haters are on a mission to defeat you in every area of your life, and their ultimate aim is to make you give up.

Chapter 2

MY STORY

It all started one day at the beginning of my 7th grade school year at Glenridge Middle School. The teacher went around the classroom asking students about their favorite hobbies and what they considered to be the most interesting occupations. At age 12, why did I say that I loved reading and working math problems as my hobby? And for an occupation, what in the world was I thinking when I told the class I was going to be a big-time entrepreneur.

From that day forward, some of the students and my so-called friends laughed and teased me every time they got a chance. They never let me forget what I said. Having big dreams and aspirations in my community was frowned upon. People took what I said as an insult. "How dare you dream?" "How dare you break the generation cycle?" "Who do you think you are?" I was told that I couldn't have money, status, an education, or enjoy the finer things in life. "That's for certain people," I was told. Who were these people?

I was ridiculed because I was different and desired a better life. I was labeled because I talked, looked, and carried myself in a different manner. Everybody wants to fit in, but I slowly came to realize that I was born to stand out. As a child, you don't know any better. But these were some hard lessons to learn. No one wants to be the butt of jokes. It's human nature to want friends who accept you for who you are—flaws and all. What I like and who I am is important to me. Today, we call this type of behavior "bullying," but back then it was called "joning" or "getting the best of someone." I cried. I got upset with myself. I asked my parents if we could move or why didn't they make more money? It got to the point where I even questioned my own existence.

After a while, pretending gets old. When I got around those people, I would downplay my enthusiasm and intelligence. I would act one way around my so-called friends and act another way when I was not around them. Ultimately, you can only do this for so long. So, I got fed up and became my own person. Yes, I lost some acquaintances and classmates, but they were not my real friends— true friends accept you for who you are.

Therefore, I learned at an early age that everybody was not for me or had my best interests at heart. I had to use these situations as learning experiences. This is when I finally decided to use what people were saying about me and how they were treating me to better myself. In other words, I learned how to use their negative comments to motivate myself to reach my maximum potential in life. My haters now became my escalators.

Chapter 3

HATERS AS ESCALATORS

An escalator is designed to move you from one level to the next. Without the significant steps in the middle (the challenges we face in life), we cannot reach our fullest potential. That's why every obstacle in life is so important. For example, babies do not walk until after they have mastered crawling and have fallen several times. The same principle applies to us. This is why every pitfall, disappointment, death, defeat, loss, roadblock, or haters are so important to the critical growth of our lives. When you try to avoid these essential steps, you impede on the progress of your growth. What would have taken you one year to master or complete may now take you several years. Your expectations have now been delayed.

I had just completed all my high school requirements in the 11th grade. During my 12th grade year in high school, I would show up for attendance and then drive to Prince George's Community College, where I completed classes during the year. When I started my first year at the University of Maryland, I took 12 credits during the summer. Combined with these summer classes and the credits I completed at the community college, I went into cruise control. Even though I was almost a sophomore, I thought I could ease up on studies and enjoy college life on campus.

But something devastating happened to me. I allowed the influence of college life and my classmates to distract me from my studies and the ultimate goal of receiving my degree. I chose to dismiss my principles and teachings. More importantly, I forgot the prayers that made it all possible. My parents then did me the biggest favor of my life—they stopped paying my tuition so that I had to get a job. Needless to say, this was an eye-opening experience. I had no one to blame but myself. All my so-called friends couldn't help me. My haters temporarily succeeded in defeating me. I believe this was the defining moment that changed the rest of my life.

Chapter 4

<u>MISTAKES</u>

Believe it or not, we all make mistakes and have made some wrong decisions in life. However, if you have not prepared or positioned yourself adequately and taken the proper steps to overcome obstacles, you will quickly lose everything and find yourself right back where you started. As fast as you reached your destination to the top, you can be on your way down. Vince Lombardi said, "It's not whether you get knocked down, it's whether you get back up."

At this time In my life, I thought everything was on target. I was 17 years old and had just graduated from high school. I was in college with grants and scholarships, and on track to complete a degree in Electrical Engineering. I had the support of my family and was having the best time of my life, driving a 1979 candy apple red Ford Pinto. I thought I had it all. But little did I know that I was on my way down.

Unfortunately, some lessons have to be learned the hard way. There is an old saying that, "you have to put in your time." This is so true. Even though our parents, guardians, and mentors try to protect or shelter us from certain elements in our lives, you know that at some point, you will have to face some tough challenges. So, it's better to face those obstacles now and battle through them, than to wait and make a bigger mess of things.

For instance, I'd rather lose $100 now due to a bad investment and learn from that mistake, rather than lose several thousand dollars later due to inexperience. Don't try to avoid or go around your lessons in life. Deal with them head on, because everybody's lesson is different. That's what makes us unique.

If you have ever played card games such as "Spades," "Uno," "I Declare War," "21," "Tunk," or "Old Maid," one thing is the same—you have to play the hand you are dealt. You can't say that you want this or that card—it doesn't work that way.

You have to make the best of what you have. It is the same way in real life—you have to embrace whatever comes your way.

Chapter 5

THE RESPONSE

In life, 90% of the way success is achieved is how we respond to the challenges that face us every day. For example, your health may fail, you may lose your job or get passed over for a promotion, you may grieve over the death of a loved one, you may experience a failed relationship or business, etc. Nonetheless, the key to overcoming these obstacles is how you respond to them. Do you sit at home looking for sympathy and have a pity party, or do you regroup, get a hold of yourself, and press forward?

You will be faced with disappointments and challenges for the rest of your life. What if you react the way most people do and complain or give up? Do you continue to hold a grudge against a person who treated you badly? Do you continue to resent the supervisor who didn't promote you or even fired you?

I tried to pick myself up and move on. After that year, I decided to enter the U.S. Army, thinking to escape or run away from my problems. Let me be the first to tell you, this did not work. At the end of the day, I still had to face my setbacks. It does not matter where you go, your problems will always be with you until you decide to fix them. So, while training in Fort Benning, Georgia (Harmony Church), I had made up my mind that when I returned home, I was going to "man up" and deal with my issues.

Again, the key component is how you respond to these challenges. If you respond in a positive way, you will get positive results. If you respond in a negative way, then you will be defeated every single time. Take your time and look for opportunities in every challenge. Look at the glass to be half full instead of half empty.

Look for progress in every situation that life brings. It's about how you view life and see yourself victorious. I don't know about you, but I look for success in every area of my life, even in the midst of my darkest challenges and setbacks. That's why I prefer to use my haters as escalators.

As mentioned earlier, everything that happened previously in your life, whether it's good or challenging, is a stepping stone to your success. I was able to learn from my failures to help me reach my goals. These are the things that define you. You have to go through something in order to get something. Here is another saying: "Nothing in, nothing out." Because of the challenges you've faced, you are now more experienced to handle your next level of adversity.

Remember, the higher you move up the ladder of success, the more challenges you'll have to overcome, so when you finally achieve your goal, you can keep it instead of losing it in a short period of time. Trust me, you will not want this to happen to you. Take heed of every opportunity that comes your way and treasure the true people or friends that cross your path.

Chapter 6

<u>THE HATRED</u>

I couldn't understand why people were treating me in such a bad way, rolling their eyes, whispering around me, or looking me up and down. I was just as normal as the next person. But because I had goals, dreams, standards, and wanted to be somebody, my classmates in high school couldn't handle it. Not only then, but even now. Once you are on top in life and you fall to the bottom, it hurts.

Certainly, it is a humbling experience that allows you to view life differently. Moreover, as I continued pursuing my studies at school, I learned to associate with people like me. The challenge was finding others with the same "I can" attitude instead of hearing "you can't." I found that many people talked the talk, but did not walk the walk.

At some point in our lives, we all need words of encouragement. We need someone to tell us "you can make it," "you can do it," "the sky is the limit," "hang in there," and "hold on." When we don't get these assurances from our family members, so-called friends, and co-workers, we must learn to overcome their negative words, fault-finding statements, and discouragements by using them as escalators.

In other words, use these words against them. Say to yourself, "The more you talk about me, the more it helps me to the next step." "The more you laugh at me, the harder I will work."

Ladies, sometimes you have to say to that man, "If you hadn't cheated on me, I wouldn't have the man of my dreams today who makes me happy."

If you hadn't hated me, I wouldn't be where I am today—successful.

If you hadn't told me that I didn't look good and was fat and ugly, I wouldn't have purchased some new clothes, lost some weight, got some contacts, changed my hairstyle, started working out, and am now looking to be America's next top model. Or, I've chosen to accept me for the way I am, and I've found someone to love me for me.

If you hadn't stood me up when I needed a ride, I wouldn't have gone out to get my own car, and because of my credit, I am now driving the luxury vehicle of my choice.

If you hadn't put me out your apartment, I wouldn't have gotten the nerve to buy my own home with a two-car garage on several acres of land.

If you hadn't told me that I wasn't smart enough and shouldn't waste my time going to college, I would never have gone back to get my GED, enrolled in college, graduated *magna cum laude*, and accepted a six-digit offer for my first job.

If you hadn't made hateful comments about me, I wouldn't have taken the necessary steps to get myself to the place I want to be in life—confident.

If you hadn't made fun of my athletic ability on the junior varsity team in high school, I wouldn't have worked extra hard over the past summer to elevate my game, gain a scholarship for college, and earn a spot on the varsity team.

If you had never told me that there was no way in the world that I could own a business, I would never have bought a franchise or started my own barber shop, insurance company, or cleaning business. And by the way, I own two businesses. This is the importance of learning how to use your negative situations and turn them into positive ones.

Sometimes, it's hard to see it coming. People would ask me, "Why are you always reading and writing?" "You're acting like a nerd." "You're no better than we are." "You might as well join us, because you will never become anything in life." Wow! When I look back over the language that my so-called friends used towards me, it's hard for me to realize how I got to where I am today. I simply used my haters as my escalators.

A.   Sports

I really enjoyed sports in middle school and high school, especially basketball. Even though I didn't play at the collegiate or professional level, I remembered what some of my teammates endured. At that age, I didn't understand everything around me. I was just having fun. However, I was smart enough to identify the unfair treatment by coaches or players on the team. In order to get adequate playing time, you were extremely talented or your parents knew the coach. However, at some point, this scheme ended up back-firing because there were students who were just as talented, but not given a chance to prove themselves. Whether or not that's fair, an opportunity should be given to those student athletes who are at practice every day, who work the hardest and who are dedicated. That's why it's a great feeling to see when a student athlete succeeds. It is success from their hard work. This is the type of reward that lasts a lifetime.

Why are you the better athlete when it comes to tennis, football, basketball, golf, volleyball, baseball, swimming, lacrosse, track and field, gymnastics, bowling, hockey, wrestling, or cheerleading? Why do you have the favor of coaches and get more playing time with better opportunities? When it's time for college, why are you the one who got chosen for a full athletic scholarship? Do not let the negative comments of your haters hinder you. If the tables were turned, your haters would flaunt it in your face. Instead, use their hatred to motivate you or your child to become the best athlete in your chosen sport.

Who was with you at 4:00 in the morning when you had to rise and start stretching and begin your workouts? Who was with you when you had to stay in and study, while everyone was dancing and having a good time at a party or attending a local gathering? Who was with you when you had to stay up late at night practicing, only to get up early the next day and start the regimen all over again? Haters only do enough to get by, but they are not willing to put in the extra work it really takes to be superlative.

This is why your haters try to convince you to quit the team and go somewhere else. Their strategy is to discourage you so they can obtain your position. Haters spread false rumors about coaches and other teammates in order to acquire someone else's position. Haters also try to talk you out of accepting a scholarship. If they can't succeed, then as an alternative, they will give you the famous "if I were you" speech. For example, "If I were you, I would not go through all the hassle." Your haters would love for you to stay home and kick it with the crew, which means becoming a bum, a product of your environment, broke, and/or another statistic of the streets. If they can't be successful, then they don't want you to succeed.

Use that hatred as a stepping stone or motivation to say, "I must be doing something right. Otherwise, I would not be getting all this attention." This is when you tell yourself, "I am going to stay here and use my haters as escalators." Use this negative energy and tell yourself, if my so-called friends and classmates hadn't hated me, I wouldn't be where I am today. As a matter of fact, I am going to work even harder.

As a father, I am experiencing this with my daughter as she excels in tennis. One would not think you would have to deal with haters at ages 10-12, but seemingly, it is just as bad. We all want our children to be the next great professional athlete, but what is the cost you are willing to pay—at the expense of degrading or crushing another child's feelings or dreams? I found that parents are putting their children through the rigors because they didn't make it themselves. Whatever happened to the days of children having fun or selecting the sport of their choice?

There is so much unbelievable and undue pressure placed on these children. I've seen many parents display this negative attitude toward their children. Since behavior is learned, the child acts out what they have seen or been taught. No wonder when the child gets ready to go to college, they don't want to have anything to do with that sport.

Nonetheless, I am teaching my daughter to always take the high road. When other girls don't want to play with her, I tell her to use that energy to her advantage. I advise her to continue to be cordial, but to use their spiteful behavior as motivation to better herself and her athletic ability. I also tell her in a positive way, when she becomes number "1," then they'll want to be her friend.

B.   Music

As a musician, it's amazing how much talent you see. It has been my experience that very few musicians are willing to share their story of how they made it to the big stage. Music is one of the most competitive and lucrative industries in the world. It is a yearly multibillion-dollar industry. A majority of individuals think they can sing or are the best musicians. This is one of the reasons *The Voice* and other music shows are so successful.

A great amount of effort goes into singing, playing instruments, harmonizing, learning vocal parts, and memorizing lyrics. The dedication and willingness to practice speaks for itself. People will try to discourage you by saying that you need to work on your breathing, technique, projection, etc. Haters will tell you that you can't sing or you don't have the professional look as the other entertainers.

Nonetheless, after it's all said and done, you really are the better singer, musician, lyrics writer, choir director, praise team worshiper, and section leader. For some reason you are hated because you were selected for the lead part or you are hated because you have a natural gift. That's okay. Shift that negative energy and push yourself to become better.

Even if you fail several times, keep pushing. Luther Vandross was booed off the Apollo Theater in New York three times. But look at what those boos did for his career. Anita Baker sent her demo out to several companies but only to be rejected and told, "not to quit her day job." Look at what the rejections did for her career. The Beatles, Ray Charles, Thomas A. Dorsey, Kirk D. Franklin, Mahalia Jackson, Michael Jackson, Elvis Presley, The Rolling Stones, and Frank Sinatra all had to overcome negativity relating to music during their distinctive eras, but look at what persistence did for them.

Ruben Studdard was sleeping in his car before he won on *American Idol*. Jennifer Hudson was singing on a cruise ship, was let go early on *American Idol*, and became homeless. But look at her now. Stop listening to negative comments from your co-workers, friends, and family.

Go out there, work hard, handle your business, and get ready to sign your multimillion-dollar contract with a recording label that will allow you to produce your own CDs. Trust me, if you have the heart, an "I can do" attitude, and you put in some good old-fashioned hard work, you will succeed.

C.   The Arts

In the arts, they try to label and prejudge you, size you up and down, and make comments like "you are too short, tall, fat, skinny, or unbalanced for this play"; "you have no coordination for this dance or choreography"; "you don't have the right look for this commercial"; "you don't have the graceful moves for this ballet piece"; "you are not what we are looking for in the next production"; etc. These are some harsh words to hear before you get the opportunity to prove yourself.

But remember, it's what's on the inside of you that counts. You may have on the right clothes, hairstyle, and necessary makeup, but when it's time to prove who you are, can you deliver? Stop looking at other people around you and focus on yourself. Turn every disadvantage into an advantage.

Say to yourself, "I may be short, but I make it up in determination. As a matter of fact, I will be in the next play." "I may be on the chunky side, but that can't stop me from dancing."

Quit looking at what you can't do and focus instead on what you do best. People spend more time telling you about your weaknesses, than encouraging you on your strengths or using their resources to help resolve your problems.

There are so many stories of famous actors and actresses who got the opportunity of a lifetime, all because they were determined to never give up. When you get a chance, read the stories of Julia Roberts, Oprah Winfrey, and Denzel Washington. That's the attitude one must have all the time in every situation. In other words, use your haters as escalators.

D.   Scholastics

Just because I had a passion for reading and working math problems, I was labeled. While this was painful, I learned to tune and block those people out of my life. People who possess a certain expertise may be labeled as "nerds" or "geeks." But every time you need help with something, you call them. When you need to prepare for an exam or write a paper, you send them a text. Every time you need to submit a proposal to your supervisor or manager, you ask for their advice. But when you are in a different environment or you are around your friends, you act like you don't know them. But that's all right. It's so ironic—you are using them for their brains.

This is what a person needs to say to overcome this type of treatment and line of thinking: "If they hadn't teased me and called me names, I wouldn't have been named valedictorian or salutatorian and received a full scholarship and ultimately the job offer of my dreams."

Haters will tell you not to read so much, it doesn't take all of that, have some fun, come party, or don't study too long. But they don't know what it took for you to get where you are. They don't know you are working on the next big successful project of your life. You are not in it for a minute, but you are making a lifetime commitment. You are working hard now so you can play hard later.

My mom and dad always told me that if you put in the time now, you will reap the benefits later. Be the best student and score as high as you can on the aptitude tests. It will certainly pay-off in the long run.

My youngest daughter and I have a saying: "We do what we have to do, so we can do what we want to do." What is it that we have to do? I am glad you asked me. We have to keep the faith, we have to work hard, we have to stay focused, we have to remain strong in spite of our obstacles, we have to give our best, and never give up.

E.   The Work Place

I value my place of employment. I was taught to be thankful for every opportunity and when you get the chance, let your employer see that you are going over and beyond to produce the best quality work product. My mindset is to bring an attitude of excellence.

As an alternative, you will find haters who do enough to meet their company's minimum level of expectation. What happened to the goal of consistently exceeding expectation? Separate yourself from these type of employees. Sometimes, you are labeled by the company you keep. If you are not careful, you will end up displaying this same negative attitude. It may mean that you need to stand alone. Let them envy you because of the outstanding job you perform. But don't let them hinder you or keep you from promotion.

You must learn to say, "Just because you come to work late, take long lunch and smoke breaks, leave early and half do your job, don't get upset with me because I made employee of the month." You worked hard to achieve your level of expertise. If they don't like their place of employment, tell them to find something else and stay out of your way.

A majority of people have negative attitudes about their jobs and want everyone else to share their sentiment. If this happens to you, quickly change your attitude and look at it as a challenge to better yourself until you receive another opportunity. Continue striving to be the best employee, work harder, arrive on time, complete the necessary training classes, go over and beyond, and find innovative ways to help the company improve.

Ultimately, help your company save money. Don't call in unless it's an emergency, and make sure your leave is scheduled and you have informed your employer in advance. If you continue to exhibit this type of positive behavior, you will be next in line for a promotion. That's why you should learn to use your haters as escalators.

As another option, you can view your employer as a lender to your dream or goal. Look at them as a means until you are in a position to open up your own business. Treat them as your largest investor. In all actuality, they are paying you to invest in your own business until you get it off the ground. You have to change your mode of thinking.

Chapter 7

WHAT IS MY GIFT OR TALENT?

I spent so much time trying to emulate others, I lost focus and wasted time trying to establish my own destiny. Many people find it difficult to determine their gift or talent. They have a hard time recognizing what they do best. I once heard Steve Harvey define your gift as, "the thing which you do best with the least amount of effort." For example, you may display a passion for playing a particular sport. However, if you need to work harder than the average player, your gift may be in athletic training, becoming a sports doctor, or sports commentating. Just because you have a passion for something doesn't necessarily mean this is your gift.

Remember, your gift or talent is something that you do better than anyone else without blinking or thinking about it. You can do it in the dark or at the push of a button. You can wake up early in the morning without any preparation, and you can start to operate. Ladies and gentlemen, this is your gift.

Take a moment to think about it. People are always asking you to help them, because they know your gift and see it inside of you. But it's time to wake up and recognize your own gift(s). I thought one thing, but it was another. Stop listening to other people and start listening to your heart.

These tools can be used to help motivate yourself to the next level. If people are not making negative comments about you, then you are not doing a good job. If everyone agrees with you and likes everything you say and do, then something is definitely wrong.

In fact, whenever someone starts the sentence off with "you think you're this or that," then you immediately know that they are envious of your gift or talent and you are on the right track.

Further, people may say something like, "you think you look nice." Then you must look like a model. "You think you are so smart." Then you must be intelligent and receive scholarly grades in school. "You think you know so much." Then you must display a wealth of knowledge. "Oh, I didn't know you were that good." They perceived your gift or talent will make room for you to be noticed in the company of great people. Let me share this secret with you—it's okay to be you. Just learn to use your haters as escalators.

Chapter 8

<u>THE TEST</u>

The first time I was introduced to my wife, the bells and whistles resonated in my heart, and I immediately knew it was love at first sight! But I didn't know anything about her. As we became friends and got to know one another, besides being stood-up on our first date, our relationship kept growing. Then, my life took a turn for the worst.

Needless to say, it was at this time in my life that my wife proved her love and commitment toward me. Some women would have said, "Let me know when you get yourself together and we can revisit our relationship." Others would have just walked away. But she encouraged and lifted me up the whole time. That was when I really knew she was the right one for me. Not when things were good, but when life was challenging.

In my opinion, this is when you find the truth about a person. Life is one test after the other. The outcome of these tests will also reveal who you can trust. Friendship is tested like everything else. There can be no test-i-mony without the "test."

For example, before you say "I do" in marriage, you need to find out if your fiancé/fiancée is compatible and in agreement with you, or is it all about them. Just because you know someone, grew up with them in the neighborhood, or worked with a co-worker for several years does not give him or her the title of friend. Friendship is earned.

Fraternities, sororities, professional athletics, cheerleaders, dancers, and singers all go through a series of tests. Friendship is no different. It needs to experience the survival from a type of trial or tribulation of time and remains unconditional.

Haters want to go to the best schools, but they do not want to adequately prepare. They want to be a professional athlete, professor, or entertainer, but they do not want to make the necessary sacrifices.

Haters want to be associated with the best organization, but are not willing to pay the price. This is the test: we all have to give up something to achieve our goals. My parents always told me that, "you don't get something for nothing" and "nothing in life is free." Ultimately, we end up learning these lessons the hard way.

In life, one of most challenging obstacles is to discover how to utilize our opportunities and transform them into achieved success. Naturally, when you get frustrated or find yourself in a difficult situation, it maybe your first instinct to give up and throw in the towel. Some will say, "Well, I guess it wasn't for me" or "I guess it wasn't meant to be." These types of individuals miss out on chances of good fortune.

Instead, we should speak words of power and conviction every day. We are what we say and believe. What comes out of your mouth determines your future. The words of your mouth have control over your life. Think about it for a minute. Now ask yourself, what have I been thinking and speaking over my life? You may realize that you have been speaking your life into or out of existence. Think big. Don't poor mouth or complain. Expect the impossible. Believe you are a winner in every area of your life and you will make a difference. More importantly, use your haters as escalators.

Chapter 9

<u>RELATIONSHIPS</u>

This is a big one. You learn so much about yourself and other people in relationships. One of the things I learned in relationships is that haters want you to be totally dependent on them. When I reflect on my past relationships, I realized I could have done things differently. There were relationships I should have worked harder to keep and others I should have walked away.

Of course, once I got hurt, I didn't want to go through that experience again. So, in order to keep this from happening, I put up my guard and vowed to never let anyone into my space or get close to me again. But after years of maturity, I got rid of this type of thinking. Ultimately, you will lose out on so many potential friends and acquaintances. Haters don't want you to be in love or in a relationship—it's all about them and no one else. Haters want you to stay single and lonely like they are. Also, it is the hater's goal to break up your happy home or relationship.

At one point in our lives, we have experienced a relationship or friendship that disappointed us. It may have led us to experience physical, emotional, or verbal abuse. For whatever reason, it left a deep scar with several bad memories. But these experiences can be a great contributor to your future. Translate that last experience as a learning tool. Get yourself together and regroup. Life is just beginning. If your fiancé/fiancée left you for another man or woman, don't beat yourself up. You can't take all the blame. Tell that man or woman that he or she missed the best thing that ever could have happened to them. Apply that energy and use it in your next relationship.

Remember, you must forgive that person, even if they did you wrong (discussed further in Chapter 17). You cannot enter into another relationship carrying unwanted baggage or holding onto issues from your past relationship. It is unhealthy and unfair to the other partner. As a result, the relationship will never succeed. Nevertheless, tell yourself that you are going to make the next one sweeter.

Ladies, if a man was physically or verbally abusing you and lowering your self-esteem, learn from that experience and turn it around. Pick yourself up and begin to live life to the fullest. Before the next relationship, recognize your insecurities and bounce back from your mistakes. Because the man of your dreams is waiting for you.

Men, if a woman was cheating on you, don't seek revenge. Stick to doing the right thing. In the long run, that person's reputation maybe tarnished, while life will more likely work out for you. Rest assured, there is a wonderful lady waiting to meet you. Since your time is precious and limited, don't waste it seeking vengeance or living someone else's dream.

For these reasons, you will never change a man or a woman. The change first starts in you. The goal is to utilize your past experiences to improve your future relationships. Occasionally, the most important lesson is to learn from your mistakes. Sometimes, it is more important to learn what not to do, instead of what to do. Moreover, continue stepping up, improving, working on you, and using your haters as escalators.

Chapter 10

<u>FAILURE</u>

First, let me say that it's okay to fail—and fail more than once. No one knows this better than me. I can't tell you how many times I've tried something and failed. Whether it was setting up a business, building a new relationship, or investing in stock prices that fell dramatically, I figured out a way to bounce back. There was something on the inside that kept telling me to get back up and try it again. So, every time I got knocked down, I got right back up, only to get knocked down again and again....

But the next time, I had more fire and determination. If someone says "no," use that "no" as a motivator. Go home, and learn how to turn that "no" into a "yes." If you get turned down by a bank, use that "no" to work on your credit and get your finances together. When you fill out the next application, hopefully, it will be a "yes." We must learn to examine every circumstance as a learning experience instead of something negative.

Remember, nothing happens overnight. Be patient. It's all about how you look at things. If you get cut from a basketball team, cheerleading team, or any other activity or sport, it is not the end of the world. Use this as motivation to enhance your skills by putting in the extra practice time, and look forward to joining the team the following year. Michael Jordan did it and now has five national basketball championship rings. Why can't you?

You may even lose your job. Use this time to go back to school, take some classes, get your certification or degree, and find the job of your dreams. Maybe this is the right time to open your own business. Things happen for a reason.

Most times, you will fail before you succeed. If you're always on top, you will never really know your true potential. Losing or failing is a humbling experience and allows you the opportunity to dig deep and find the hidden treasure and truths inside of you. One becomes a better employee after they get passed over a position they thought belonged to them. You become a better cook when the dish does not turn out the way you expected. These are growing pains. Just because you failed two or three times does not mean it's over. In fact, you may fail 10 or more times until you get it right.

All this means is that you need to work harder and put in some additional time. Failures help to define who we are. It also helps us to become the best we can be. We need to fail so that we can get better. Remember, before you learn how to walk, you will fall several times. There has to be a mixture of rain and sunshine for the plant to grow. Without the rain, the plant dies—and so do we. This is a way of showing us that there is more in store for us, if we just keep the faith, work hard, and hold on.

No matter how many mistakes you make, how many times you fail, or how slow you progress, you are still "way ahead" of everyone who isn't trying.

Chapter 11

SELF-ESTEEM

Self-esteem is so important. It is essential because it reveals what you think about yourself. If you don't believe in yourself, then who will? Haters will tease you and make you feel degraded. Haters will make you think that you are too big, too skinny, too fast, too slow, or too ugly; you don't dress well; you are uneducated; your complexion is too light or dark skinned; you don't have enough money or your car is a bucket; or they ridicule where you live, your name, the school you attended, or your parent's occupation.

Material things are so insignificant when it comes to defining who you are. Whatever the case, it's the hater's goal to make you feel less than a person. It is also the hater's goal to make you give up on your dreams. You have to learn how to respond to this kind of hatred. The quicker you learn this, the better off you will be and the faster you can get started on reaching your dreams and goals.

Easier said than done, right? I always felt that other people were better than me. Also, it appeared to me that these same people were more gifted and talented. As a matter of fact, haters will always try to make you feel that you are beneath them, when in actuality, you are superior. That is part of their tactic—to not let you think you better qualified. My mentor worked with me on building my self-esteem and helping me to believe in me. He helped me to realize that I was just as important, talented, smarter, more athletic, and gifted as they were. I began to realize that, with some hard work and dedication, I can be great.

You have to change your level of thinking about yourself. I would always put myself down when I compared myself to others. I made negative comments about myself and downplayed my aspirations. I'd say things like, "I wish it were me." "Maybe one day I can do that." "Good things never happen to me."

Who wants to hear that all the time? Even though we are created to look at others, it's difficult to take a good hard look at yourself in the mirror. That's why it's so easy to tell someone else what to do or not to do. But when it's time to make a decision about yourself, you can't figure it out. Believe it or not, you have what it takes and more.

I know it's difficult to change after years and years of being told how inadequate you are and phrases like, "You will never make it." "You are not worthy." "You can't do it." "You don't have what it takes." "We need someone with more experience." "You are incompetent." "You will never learn this in time." "You will end up like the rest of us." "You're just like your father."

As a substitute, defend your values and principles when met with opposition. Trust your own judgment and don't feel guilty when others don't like your choice. Don't lose sleep worrying about the past, nor about what could happen in the future. The goal is to learn from the past, plan for the future, but live in moment, which is the present. In the end, trust yourself.

Chapter 12

FREE YOURSELF FROM PEOPLE

This particular topic is one of the most challenging because people cherish their relationships. For various reasons, we care what people think and say about us. It's hard for us to forget about our family, neighbors, co-workers, and friends. We have a tendency to think that we owe them something. Yes, I know it takes a village to raise a child. But if you have not been a part of the village, what do I owe you? This is why I couldn't move to the next level. I was too busy trying to please and satisfy everyone else, I forgot about me—the most important person. I had to come to a point in my life where it didn't matter what people thought or said.

The more important question is, was I doing it for me? Russell Simmons wrote a book entitled, "Do You!" Mr. Simmons listed 12 laws to access the power in you to achieve happiness and success. When it's all said and done and you ask people for help, everybody has an excuse or something else to do. That's because they have been hating you all along. But once you make it in to the USTA, NBA, NFL, MLB, Kennedy Center, Carnegie Hall, or Congress, or become a dean, CEO, or CFO, everybody, including your haters, will have their hands out wanting something from you. Stop using people as your excuse and use them as escalators.

Haters will do everything they can to hold you back from your dreams and goals. If you were a bird, they would clip your wings to prevent you from flying. You may not perceive it now, but either your wings have already been clipped, or someone is currently trying to clip them. But if you don't recognize you are an eagle, people will treat you like a bird. So, if you expect to fly and soar high like the eagle, you must get rid of some people in your life. Then you will capitalize on the fact that you were entertaining birds, but should be flying with eagles.

Chapter 13

FREE YOURSELF FROM YOURSELF

Sometimes hatred comes from inside of you. You have to let up on yourself. Most importantly, you have to be true to yourself. Make sure you are doing it for yourself and not everybody else. During this period in my life, I thought I should be further than where I was. I began to compare myself to others instead of accepting my unique state of being. I looked at people's age, social economic status, degrees, and their material belongings.

Of course, when I compared myself to others, I ended up putting myself down. Once you look back over your life, you will realize this type of thinking is a waste of time and energy. Don't hate or beat yourself up by comparing yourself to someone else. Finally, I learned to love myself for who I am and what I have to offer.

We all peak at different times. Just because someone peaks earlier than you, does not mean that you will not catch up with them later or even surpass them. That's why it's better to be an original than a copy. Will the real you please stand up and take control? There is only one President Barack Obama. Who are you going to be? There is only one Hillary Clinton. Who are you going to be? There is only one Julia Roberts or Arthur Ashe. Who are you going to be?

This also applies to people who mentor you, or to people you admire or would like to emulate. We don't always know the true path of their success or what it took for them to get to where they are. We only know what portion they decide to share. It could be a false impression. That's why it is important to love yourself and be confident in who you are. You can't be a hater of yourself. If you are, you are no good to anyone—especially yourself. It all starts within you, by transforming and renewing your mind.

Some people judge themselves based on the material possessions of others or what they think about them. If we don't have the same things, we beat ourselves up. We look at what other families are doing, such as where they live, what they drive, where they vacation, what they do, and where they send their kids to school. This even goes on in our relationships.

We compare our relationships to others, instead of doing what's right for our own. Needless to say, you can have all that stuff and still be miserable. Accept who you are and know when it's your time, you will have everything you need and desire. Free yourself from you. Because you can be a major stumbling block, barrier, or hurdle for your own success.

Marianne Williamson wrote a poem entitled, "Our Deepest Fear." The summary of this poem talks about an individual who fears becoming powerful, great, and surpassing others. Think about this for a moment. What would you do or become if you were able to live in a world without fear? Your answer should be–anything. Try to live without fear for 30 days and see what happens. Repeat these words: "Perfect love casts out all fear." It helps me to realize that my potential is unlimited. Once you fully believe, you will overcome the perception of doubts or failure. The goal is to push past any limitations, dream big, and soar high to the level of your desired achievement. If you do, you'll discover some unique and great hidden secrets about yourself. So, use your haters as escalators, even if it means you.

Chapter 14

SHARING SUCCESS WITH OTHERS

It was hard for some of my friends to accept. But it didn't bother me. I found my way back. I bought my first condo, completed college, landed a job, got married, and was working on my graduate degrees. All of a sudden, the hate came. I was still the same person, but with regards to life, we were going in different directions. Where was the love? Unfortunately, I lost some friends because they could not handle my personal accomplishments.

This was unsettling because we grew up affirming that whatever each of us accomplished, we would share it with each other. I knew the importance of sharing, because I experienced falling to the bottom during one point in my life. And now that I was in a position to assist others, my circle of so-called friends did not want my help. Instead of celebrating with me, I was ignored and made to feel like I had done something wrong. I was told, that I thought I was "this and that." It hurt, but eventually, I got over it and moved on.

When you are sharing your success with others, don't expect them to feel the same way you do. Be cautious! It's clear that you definitely now what you want from life and are on the right track. However, when you are sharing good news about your progress, promotion, engagement, job, new home, car, church, baby, or special moments, don't get upset when their response is not equivalent to your expected level of excitement. Everybody can't handle your success. This is when you feel the negative tension, energies and thoughts towards you. In fact, you will be able to identify your true friends. And if you lose some friends as a result, they weren't your real friends anyway. Once it's all over, some will stop speaking, visiting, and hanging out with you. They will begin to tell others that you think you are arrogant and snobbish. In reality, you will find out they are jealous and are your true haters.

Chapter 15

BUZZ WORDS

When things were not going my way, I needed something to spark or trigger an alternative way of thinking. I yearned for words to inspire me. Athletes do it all the time. When they are trying to turn things around, they ball up their fists and figure out a way to get motivated by screaming out positive words or affirmations. Therefore, I began to use buzz words to fuel my energy to succeed.

The old saying is that "sticks and stones may break my bones, but names will never hurt me."

Somehow, we let these names hurt us. We believe it and feel sorry for ourselves. Instead, try this: "sticks and stones may break my bones, but names and words will always help me." Your haters don't know it, but every time they say something negative about you, they are giving you a compliment. Every time they do something to destroy your self-esteem, they are providing you with the tools and motivation to conquer your enemies. For example:

You think you are something. Evidently, your haters know you are in the process of achieving something great. Otherwise, your haters would not have wasted their energy to say something.

She thinks she's cute. She must be gorgeous.

He thinks he's got it going on. He does.

He's got a new job and doesn't have time for us now. When you get to a certain level, you have to cut the negative people out of your life and get some new friends. Of course, you should never forget where you come from, but at the same time, you cannot forget where you are going. Here are some more sayings to think about:

She thinks she can sing. She definitely has the voice of an angel.

He thinks he can make it in the NFL. He must be an awesome football player.

All she does is talk about owning her own business. Apparently, they see she is on the verge of owning her own hair salon, franchise, or company. This happens all the time. People see your dream, sometimes, before you do.

Here is another one. They always act like they are in love. Seemingly, they make a beautiful couple—a match made in heaven. Also, these haters can't find anyone to love them the same way someone loves you.

Don't you already have a house and a car? They are still trying to get out of momma's house.

You just got back from another vacation. Your haters can't go on vacation, because they spend too much money trying to keep up with the Jones's. Remember, misery loves company.

Ladies and gentlemen, folks can't handle your success or dreams! Another mentor told me that if someone believes in your dream, then you haven't dreamed big enough. When someone tells you that your dream is too big or impossible, then you know you are on the right track!

Chapter 16

WHATEVER

There are many facets of life we experience, but don't have answers. Everyone is going to go through something. It could be hard times, disappointments, final exam, divorce, homelessness, prison, suicide, or trying to figure out your next move, etc. So be prepared.

This is why it is so important to respond to life positively. Let me share another secret with you about the word "whatever." The word "whatever" has another meaning that can be interpreted as "no matter what happens." It is used as a response implying indifference. For instance, whatever you throw at me to keep me down, I am going to rise.

Dr. Maya Angelou wrote a poem entitled, "Still I Rise." In so many words, Dr. Angelou talked about different circumstances a person may endure in life. In other words, Dr. Angelou encouraged the reader not to be frustrated with obstacles, but to rise at every setback and disappointment. Whatever names you call me do not hurt, because I rise. Whatever frown you give me, I am going to smile. Whatever lies people tell, the truth will come forth. Whatever way you treat me, I am going to show you love.

One of my favorite sayings is that "I am going to act like a duck and let the water roll off my back." I don't have time to worry about things I cannot change. But I can change myself and how I respond. Whatever is on my exam, I am going to ace it. Whatever they tell me I cannot do, I'll make it a point to accomplish. Whatever the size of my mountain, I will speak to it—so it can be removed. Whatever the darkness of my situation, light is at the end of the tunnel. Whatever looks impossible, I know it can come to fruition. Whatever my start looks like, does not determine my future. Whatever prognosis the doctor gives, I am going to live and not die, because I am healed. Whatever my finances are currently, does not determine my wealth later. Whatever sentence the judge proclaims, it can be overturned. Whatever my broken relationship feels like at the moment, it will not remain the same—it will be restored.

Whatever, whatever, whatever—I am victorious in every area of my life. Say "whatever" to those circumstances or obstacles that are trying to keep you down and suppressed. Whatever comes your way, rest assured, you are an overcomer. If it worked for me; it will work for you. Use your haters as escalators.

Chapter 17

FORGIVENESS

I believe one of the hardest things to accept in life is to forgive people who abused or hurt you physically, verbally, or spiritually in the past. There is so much anger and bitter feelings that accumulates over the years. But in order to continue ahead in life, you must let it go. Don't let this be a hindrance.

You don't need any extra weight holding you down, nor do you want anyone to have that type of control over your life. While it is natural to feel angry, revenge puts you on the same level with those spiteful people. Instead, channel your energy to be more productive. Since your attitude determines your altitude, forgiveness liberates you from negativity and allows you to move forward.

One day, I drafted a list of people who were dishonest to me. After much thought, I finally decided to seek a morally superior approach and forgive each and every person. Words can't explain how I felt after this "feat." Oh, what a relief! As a matter of fact, I made it a point to contact every person on my list. When I did get the opportunity to see them or speak to them again, I was able to overcome feelings of rage, cross them off my list, and enjoy the freedom of healed wounds. I didn't want to have anything in my heart against anyone because I believe that nothing can replace the experience of inner peace, love, health, and happiness in your life.

As a testament, the life and legacy of South African President Nelson Mandela taught people how liberating it is to forgive. Although he had served in a South African prison for 27 years, he sought unification for his country rather than revenge on the people who had put him in jail. In other words, he mastered using his haters as escalators.

Chapter 18

THANK YOU

Did anyone ever tell you that you will never make it or be successful in life? I was told this several times. But I just kept believing in myself. I knew something better was coming my way. I didn't know how or when—I just had a feeling that everything would be all right. In high school, there was a schoolmate who made fun of everybody. Every day during lunch period, we all sat around the table in the cafeteria and he would begin to make fun of people until it hurt someone.

It was always funny until they started laughing at me. Yes, I laughed and went along with everyone, but on the inside it felt like I was hemorrhaging. I then understood how the other students felt by these insults. It really hurt. But what could I do? If I had gone to the teacher, it would have been his word against mine. I certainly couldn't tell my classmates. They would have thought less of me. I could have felt self-pity, or I could have used those negative statements and turned them into positive steps. Needless to say, I chose the latter.

About 28 years later, I got an opportunity to see him again. This particular Saturday morning, while running errands, I visited a different car wash. I thought I had noticed a familiar face among the employees, but I was unsure and did not recognize him until he called me by name. His head was down because he was now washing my car. It's amazing how life has a way of turning things around. We exchanged pleasant greetings as we were happy to see one another, because it had been several years.

When I got ready to go, I told him, "Thank you for everything." He said, "For the car wash?" I said, "No, if it hadn't been for your insults at the lunch table years ago, I would never have built up the courage and self-confidence today."

He said to me, "One day, I knew you would become somebody, that's why I ragged on you so much. I was jealous and didn't know how to ask for help or get out of my negative environment. Since, the only thing I was good at was comedy and talking about other people, I didn't take the time to use my talent in a positive way. Instead, I got caught up in the wrong crowd and made people laugh at any cost." Of course, I encouraged him not to give up, but to do it the right way. This is a perfect example of how people can hate you, yet not knowing how to handle you.

Once you succeed, call the person who made those negative statements and say "thank you." "If you hadn't lowered my self-esteem, I would never have gotten myself together to become the success I am today."

Even though some of the hater's statements might be true, a reality check from these statements might get us to think about making a positive change in our lives. This could be the turning point to get your life back on track.

When I first got into the military, I remember making the first allowed call to my dad to thank him for the discipline, never giving up on me, and being the best dad a son could acclaim. All along, I thought he was mean, didn't care, and was just a hard task master. Needless to say, I didn't know that all his corrections and punishments were preparing me for life and made me the person I am today. For me, tough love was the best love. It saved my life. Make that telephone call and let that special someone know you appreciate them. Even though they were hating you on the inside, they may respond with something like, "I was just trying to push you. I knew you could do it." Yeah, right—whatever!

Use these statements to make up your mind that you are going to be successful in spite of the obstacles and ridicule. Say to yourself that you are going to use your haters as escalators.

Chapter 19

<u>WORDS OF ENCOURAGEMENT</u>

Whatever circumstances you face in life, don't give up on your dreams or goals. Every morning when you wake up, tell yourself that you are another day closer to success. Every day is a great day, because it is a day that the Lord has made. Trust me—whatever the Lord makes is great. Never say this is a bad day. You may have a challenging day or you may be tested that day. It's similar to saying you woke up on the wrong side of the bed. Whatever side you wake up is the right side. It's great to wake up and be alive. My grandmother said to me on several occasions, "It's a blessing to be in the land of the living one more time." I truly understand now. In other words, we all get 24 hours each day. The difference is what you do with yours.

It's up to you to make the best of life and all its opportunities. Tell yourself that you are "fearfully and wonderfully made." Keep telling yourself: "I am awesome." "I am the best at what I do." "Today is going to be the best day of my life." "It starts right here, right now." "If I can't be happy where I am, I can be happy where I want to be." "My dream is not a New Year's resolution, it's a lifetime commitment." "I'm not another statistic." "The right time for me to start is now." "I am the first in my family to attend college." "I am the first in my family to open up a business." "I am the first in my family to travel, be a doctor or a lawyer."

"I am the next '_____'" (you fill-in the blank)!

In spite of what people say, think, or feel about you, hold fast to what you believe. For those who believe, "all things work together for your good." Everything happens for a reason, so spend time listening, thinking, and reasoning. Don't dismiss your haters. Refuse to avoid, go around, or over them.

Instead, embrace them directly. This is the place where you will find the answer to some of your problems. If you keep the faith and persevere, your determination will create a path through these obstacles and help you overcome any haters. Sometimes you have to say, "You may be on top now, but just wait and see; the best is yet to come."

I once believed that haters were a true sign of my failure as inferred by the old cliché, "It's not meant to be." This is a big misconception. In the midst of my storms, I've learned to appreciate my haters to a greater extent. If it wasn't for my haters, I wouldn't be where I am today. My haters and my circumstances in life have made me stronger, wiser, better educated, successful, and a happier person today. I finally learned to use my haters as escalators.

Chapter 20

SUMMARY

The overall mission of this book is really dedicated to help people transition through their past and use their current situations in life to achieve their goals. When I look back over my experiences in elementary school, middle school, high school, and college, every lesson I learned prepared me for greatness today. If I can do it, you can, too. We must stop making excuses for the hands that we are dealt in life. Instead, use these situations as the foundations for building your dreams and moving to the level of achievement you desire. Stop procrastinating about what you were born to contribute in society. Do something about it. You can't control what happens to you, but you can control how you respond. The solution is inside of you. You may not see the whole staircase of your life, but if you take the first step, you are one step closer to your dreams.

Most often, these unexpected challenges initiate the process that pushes and motivates us. Somehow, we are then forced to use our gifts or talents to the best of our abilities. Despite our life's circumstances and the negative influences we receive from others, we must learn to "use our haters as escalators."

I hope you were encouraged by reading my life changing experiences to make a difference in your life. Please share this book with others, as over 1 million copies, in different translations, will be sold to help people overcome life's obstacles all over the world.

CONTACT INFORMATION

If you are interested in booking Dr. Sampson for any speaking engagements, interviews, or seminars, please feel free to contact his office: (1) via phone on 240.472.7786, (2) via email: ferronnie@verizon.net.; or (3) tweet him @DrFerRonnieS on Twitter.

www.ingramcontent.com/pod-product-compliance
Lightning Source LLC
LaVergne TN
LVHW011339080426
835513LV00006B/434